Davina + Quinn
a short story

Love's Farewell

Deborah Armstrong

ISBN paperback: 978-1-989747-07-0
ISBN eBook: 978-1-989747-08-7
ISBN audio: 978-1-989747-09-4

Cover, interior and eBook conversion:
Rebecca Finkel, FPGD.com

To order additional copies of this book, contact:
Deborah@deboraharmstrong.ca or
TerrahillPublishing@gmail.com

author's note

When I finished the Davina and Quinn series, it was hard to say goodbye to the characters I spent so much time with and loved. They still send me ideas and stories they want me to write on their behalf. Instead of writing another novel, I decided to write short stories. These stories focus on a singular event that profoundly affects the characters.

The first of the short stories is *Love's Farewell* featuring Davina and Quinn Thomas (my two lovers in the Davina and Quinn series) and Foxx O'Connell, the semi-villain in *Love's Games.* I'll let my readers decide Foxx's level of badness. In this short story, Foxx asks Davina for a final favour she feels bound to grant.

This story is not a romance, although love is one of the themes. It is a story about death and dying and leaving this world surrounded by our loved ones.

I welcome you if you are new to the Davina and Quinn series. This short story will give you insight into Davina and

Quinn, who love passionately and unconditionally. Their love story has many twists and turns, keeping readers on their toes.

If you want to learn more about this series, I've included my book covers along with a brief synopsis for each book.

I invite you to check my website and follow me on social media. Sign up for my weekly newsletter to receive delicious romantic recipes and my *Friday Feel-Good* blog.

Happy reading,

Deborah

Quinn

one

What does it say about a man who, for purely selfish reasons, wishes for another man's death?

I am a selfish bastard. I am not ashamed to admit it. When it comes to my wife and family, they are mine, and I will protect them with everything in my power. I will fight for them with my dying breath. And there's the irony of it. The man whose speedy death I wish for wants to spend his last breath with my wife. How can I deny him that when that is precisely how I would like to leave this world?

When she first told me about his request, my immediate response to Davi was to say no. One doesn't say no to my wife. Not that she's spoiled and used to getting her way. Far from it. She's always right. It's one of the things I love about her, even though it's the most frustrating thing about her. After sixteen years of marriage, I should know enough not to argue with her, to let her follow her heart, and yet my heart tells me to hold on to her as tight as I can because if I let her go, she may never return.

We sit in her office having our afternoon coffee break. It's our time to discuss our day and our various projects. We think of it as our quiet hour before the kids return from school. Sometimes we skip coffee altogether and spend the hour in bed. Today, I wish we were in bed instead of discussing Foxx O'Connell. We argue quietly and calmly because that's how my wife wins every damned time.

"Foxx needs me."

"Your place is here with me and our kids," I reply from the comfort of my old leather armchair as I watch her from across her desk. "We need you."

"I won't deny him, Quinn. I owe him. We both owe him for all that he's done for us."

"It's not appropriate. You're my wife. Doesn't he have someone else to sit by his deathbed? I'm putting my foot down on this, Davina Stuart Thomas. I'm your husband. My wants should take precedence over his." I use her full name when she ignites a fire in my gut that always works its way down to my groin.

Her head lowers, and she gives me that look, the one where her beautiful blue eyes turn a deep sapphire, warning me that I've crossed the line. She sees that I'm playing with my wedding band. I know I am done for before she speaks words that will cut me deeper than the polished silver letter opener lying on top of today's unopened mail.

"If I remember correctly, dear husband, you wanted nothing more than to wear my ring so that you could show the world that you belonged to me. It was also your wants that put all of us in a terrible mess—one that Foxx was kind enough to help me through. He may have had a plan, but Foxx has always been a friend to me. He stepped up when you refused to. I shouldn't need to remind you of that. And I won't be lectured on how to act appropriately, especially by you."

She never brings up the past unless I force it upon her. She forgives me, although we will never forget what happened. Our son, David, is a constant reminder of the consequences of my wants, and although we love him dearly, it is I who have never been able to shake off the shame of my actions.

"Damn it, Davi!"

"Foxx has no one else. No family. No friends close enough to offer to be by his side. He has asked for me, and I will honour his request. It's only for a few days, and I can give him that. I will give him that."

She gets to her feet and walks around the desk to join me. She offers her hand to me, and I take it hungrily, as though she were delivering a bone to a starving, lovesick dog. I pull her onto my lap. She makes herself comfortable, clasping her hands around my neck.

"There's no need to be jealous," she says softly, comforting me. "Foxx was never a threat to you. He still isn't."

"I'm not jealous of him. I'm jealous of what you are giving him." I see that look in her eyes, the one she gives only to me. "You think I'm an idiot, don't you?" I can feel the tightness in my chest begin to ease as my cock hardens. She knows how to get to me every damned time.

"No, but if you are an idiot, you are *my* idiot."

She lifts her face to me, offering me a kiss. It's a soft kiss she gives me. I want more, and I pull her in tighter, my mouth covering hers, my tongue tasting her delicious mouth. Her body softens against mine, her pleasure evident in the soft hum she makes.

I want her. My hands find the hem of her T-shirt and slip underneath it. Her skin is soft and warm. She's always warm. Always ready for me.

My mind gives me options for making love to my wife in a nanosecond. On her desk, in this chair, or on the soft carpet at our feet. Papers and half-full coffee mugs cover the desk. The rug is close and convenient. I want to have her underneath me, so the carpet wins.

Davi holds on as I move to the floor, our kiss unbroken. She releases me, her hands working on her pants, pulling them down over her hips to give me access. I fumble with my belt, then my zipper. I work my jeans past my ass, giving me enough freedom to get down to business. We have to be fast. The kids will be home in ten minutes.

Fifteen if we're lucky.

Davi reaches for my head. Her fingers run through my hair, causing my erection to jerk. "Hurry," she says, almost breathless when she releases me from our kiss. "Fast and furious, stud."

Fuck. My wife wants me to bang the hell out of her, and I know that's what I have to do, what I want to do because she owns me, and I give her whatever she needs. And our kids will be home soon, and we don't want them to see this.

She arches her back as I thrust into her. I clench my jaw. She's tight. I move my hips, working my way inside her, stretching her. She pulls my hair. Her hips move with mine. She's fucking me as hard as I am her.

"Harder."

I groan—beads of sweat form on my forehead. I strain against my jeans, cursing that I didn't kick them off. The floor hurts my knees. I'm too old for this, but I don't care. My wife wants me inside her. She loves me even though I'm a jealous prick—her jealous prick.

It's as though she can read my mind. Davi takes my face in her hands and pulls me closer to her. She smiles and says, "You're mine. Forever."

I lose it. I come hard and fast. Her soft cry of release joins my hard moan. I collapse and bury my face into Davi's neck. My ragged breath is hot against her skin. Her hands go underneath my shirt, and I feel their soft caress. She gives me time to get myself together and then reminds me of the time by patting me on the back.

I grunt my displeasure while realizing her discomfort—this rug doesn't give the floor much padding for sex. I get to my feet and pull up my pants. She holds out her hand to me, and I help her up. I watch her while she adjusts her clothing. The slight blush on her face and messy hair are signs that she just had sex. I wonder if our kids will notice. My T-shirt clings to my sweat-soaked chest.

Of course they will. They aren't idiots like their father.

Davi runs her fingers through her hair while she returns to her desk. She retrieves lipstick from the top drawer and applies it expertly to her lips without using a mirror. I marvel at how easily my wife does that. Then she sits in her chair and motions for me to sit in mine.

Everything is back to normal as we wait for the sound of our children's arrival. We both reach for our coffee mugs and sip the now-cold brews.

Davi gazes at me and says, "I'm leaving tomorrow."

Davina

two

Quinn made love to me twice this morning. I knew what
he was doing, and I let him. I don't understand his insecurity
when it comes to us. I would never leave him, yet he sees
every man I meet as a potential threat. While driving to Foxx's
cottage, Quinn wanted to make sure that I would think of him,
still feeling the tingle from two spectacular orgasms. I don't
need an orgasm to think of Quinn, and I won't be the one to
let him in on that secret.

Haliburton is a three-hour drive from our home. Quinn
didn't trust the weather or the roads to be safe at this time of
year, and rightly so. He insisted that I have a driver. I didn't
make a fuss. I looked forward to having someone else drive
and keep me company.

Josh is one of our regular drivers. His girlfriend is visiting
her mother in Australia for a month, making him the perfect
choice for accompanying me. He knows me well enough to
know when I need some conversation or quiet. Today is a day
for light conversation.

He gets out of the Cadillac SUV and gives the nod and a respectful "Sir" to Quinn, who stands with me at the kitchen doorway.

The expression on Quinn's face is severe. What an actor! I nudge him with my elbow. "Say hi to Josh, sweetheart."

"Hello, Josh. The roads might be slick. Drive with care today."

"As always," Josh answers as he takes the cooler from Quinn and delivers it to the trunk of the waiting vehicle.

I've packed the cooler with homemade stew, baking, and other goodies—more than enough to last the weekend. I have the feeling that I won't be in Haliburton for long.

"Call me. Anytime." Quinn's voice is low and full of emotion. "I'll be waiting to hear from you." He takes me in his arms and kisses me. He gives me his kiss, the toe-curling only-for-me kiss that has rocked my world all these years and leaves me breathless.

When he releases me, all I can do is smile. He knows I'll call him.

I turn and head for the waiting vehicle. Josh takes my overnight bag from me and opens the back door for me.

"I'm riding shotgun today," I announce as I stop beside the front passenger door.

Josh gives me that look that tells me Quinn isn't going to like it. It's against the rules. Quinn has standards for me and how I travel.

I smile as Josh opens the door and helps me into the Cadillac. "It's okay," I say as I wave to Quinn. "I told him before you arrived. Why else do you think he's cranky?"

A large Tim Horton's coffee cup is in the cup holder, and I'd bet a banana walnut muffin is in the little paper bag on the armrest. I look out the window and blow a kiss to Quinn. No matter how upset he is with me, my incredibly jealous man will always look after me.

Josh and I pass the time talking about various Netflix shows, the worst Christmas gifts we ever received, and Hollywood gossip. I may not be a fan of the Hollywood scene, but it doesn't mean I don't keep up on the latest dirt. Quinn isn't one to gossip, but our close-knit group of friends south of the border make sure to keep me up to date.

Our driving time passes quickly.

I shift my body seat and gaze out the window at the snow-covered landscape. The fir tree branches sag under the weight of the newly-fallen snow. I can't help but think that the dull grey of the sunless sky is providing an ominous warning of what is waiting for us. I'm sure Josh can sense the tension growing in me. He speaks only to confirm directions as we travel along dirt-covered roads to arrive at a narrow lane recently cleared of snow.

I had visited Foxx's cottage once before, many years ago. I was surprised that I knew the way as though I had been there yesterday. The cottage looked as I remembered it, plain in the front with no distinguishing features.

Oh, but the back…

The back view was magnificent, with floor-to-ceiling windows overlooking a spectacular lake. Although I'd spent a mere three days here, the picture remained etched permanently in my memory.

Josh puts the car in park and then turns off the engine. I know he's watching me as I gaze at the cottage, giving me time to take all of this in. I never thought how strange this must feel to him, accompanying me to be with another man who was dying. He is probably wondering where he would stay, how he would pass the time, or, more likely, what Quinn was thinking to let me come here.

"There's a guest bedroom for you. It has Wi-Fi and a TV."

"Anything's fine," he answers. He's a professional. This trip isn't about his comfort.

I take Josh's hand and squeeze it. "Thank you for being here, Josh. I know this may be uncomfortable for you. I bet you never thought this was part of your job description."

"It's okay. Don't give it another thought." He points toward the cottage. "Are you ready?"

I nod my answer and then wait for him to open my door for me. Even when Quinn isn't around, I sit and wait. We all respect his standards. The little things he ensures others do for me constantly remind me how much he is a part of my life. He is always with me.

How can he doubt that?

XO XO XO

Foxx O'Connell was meticulous in everything he did, so it was not surprising when he told me he had planned every detail for his final days.

I first knew him as my editor for my debut novel, *Second Harvest*. We were opposites, drawn immediately to each other. He was stylish in his appearance, whereas I was happy to wear jeans and T-shirts. He loved city life, and I was the country girl who visited the city on rare occasions. Our love of the written word, getting lost in the world of prose, was the basis of our bond. And then, Rene and David were thrown into our mix, pulling us closer together.

The cottage was Foxx's escape from the city. It was nothing like how he showed himself to the world. The furniture, perfect for cottage life, could be sat on whether one's clothes were wet or dry. The old wood floor had a few coloured throw mats; its cleaning was a sweep-out every morning. Plates and cutlery didn't match, including coffee mugs—his finds at garage sales while en route to the cottage. There was an immediate sense of welcoming as soon as I entered this place. There was no need for that to change, especially today.

A man dressed in sweat pants and a hoodie greets us at the door. "You must be Ms. Stuart. Foxx told me you were beautiful. He wasn't wrong."

I smile, and it doesn't escape my attention that Foxx still won't use my married name. Even now, approaching death, he's still a stubborn jackass.

He stands back to let us come inside. "I'm Foxx's nurse, Evan."

"He sent a bodyguard! Still the same old jealous prick." Though weaker than I'm used to, a familiar voice calls out to me from a hospital bed set up in the living room.

"This is Josh. He's not my bodyguard. He's my driver. Quinn didn't want me driving the back roads alone. He was thinking of my safety."

I take off my boots and hand my coat to Evan. "How is he?"

He nods in Foxx's direction. "He's comfortable. He's been waiting for you."

"I'm not gone yet!" Foxx calls out to us.

"Good. I'd hate to think I drove here and missed the main event," I answer him. "Although Quinn wouldn't have minded." I wink at Evan.

"How is that self-absorbed, controlling son of a bitch?"

I move to take the bags into the kitchen. Josh and Evan wave me off and gesture for me to go to Foxx.

"He's still the love of my life," I say to him as I approach. "He sends his best."

"Meaning, hurry up and die, no doubt." Foxx is sitting up in bed. A brightly-coloured quilt with a starburst pattern covers him. His face is gaunt, and his red hair is perfect, smoothed back in his usual style. His eyes are still bright, and they put me at ease.

Foxx gives me a weak smile.

"No comment." I lean down and kiss Foxx on his forehead. His skin is cool to the touch. "I won't ask you how you are. Just promise to tell me if you need anything."

"I promise."

I take the seat beside his bed and take his hand. "This place has a gorgeous view."

Foxx nods his head in agreement.

"When did you winterize it?"

"Last year. When I found out I was sick, I wanted this view to be the last thing I saw besides your face."

I swallow hard. Foxx was never one to hold back on the charm, and there was no reason to think he would now. I let his words hang in the air, unable to shoot them down.

He continues to speak, "Facing one's mortality can cause one to make plans. Wills, insurance, how to die—"

"Not many of us get to choose how we die." I'm not ready to talk about death. Not yet. "Remember when we sat out on the deck and listened to the cry of the loons?"

Foxx nodded. "Some nights, you can hear the wolves howling."

"You have wolves here?"

"Up in the highlands, there's a pack. The wind carries their calls down through the trees when the air is just right."

"That must be wonderful to hear."

"It is."

We sit in comfortable silence. I let my gaze take in the large room. The furniture is close together to allow room for the hospital bed. And yet, it still seems cozy, especially with the fire burning in the stone fireplace. Classical music plays softly in the background, and a few candles burn, giving off a light scent. I wait for Foxx to speak.

"Did you ever wonder about us? What might have been if Rene and Quinn had made things work?"

"Yes, I did."

A smile crosses Foxx's face, and he laughs. "You're a terrible liar, Davi. You never could tell a lie to save your life."

"I don't know how you know that," I say with mock indignation.

"Because I'm an expert liar, and I can tell when I hear a lie." He pats my hand. "You've only loved him. He doesn't deserve you. Neither do I, and yet both of us live for any scrap you throw our way."

His words take my breath away. I gaze at him in disbelief.

"You're beautiful and smart, yet you have no concept of what you do to men." His gaze searches my face for understanding.

"Your dying is no excuse for you to be cruel." I get to my feet and head to the window. It's mid-afternoon, and the sky is still dull. I marvel at the contrast made by the whiteness of the snow-covered ground leading to the lake's shore. At this moment, I almost wish I could be swallowed up by the snow and be anywhere but here, but I don't because I know there is truth to what Foxx says.

"I don't mean to be cruel."

"I'm not responsible for what Guy Tremblant did." I turn to face him. "Please don't put that on me."

"Christ! Davi, I was trying to compliment you, not piss you off."

Foxx closes his eyes and grimaces. I wonder if it's cancer causing him pain or remembering that I almost died at the hands of a man obsessed with me. He takes in a deep breath and then lets it out slowly. I wait for him to open his eyes.

"Damn it. I swear the thought of that bastard never crossed my mind. I'm sorry."

"It's okay. Don't give that man any more of your time. He doesn't deserve it." I make my way to him and take his hand once more. "Why don't we start over? No more talk about the men in my life unless their name is David or Jack. Deal?"

Foxx squeezes my hand. "Deal." He relaxes and settles into his pillow. "Where are my manners? Would you like something to drink or eat?"

"I'm fine. Josh and I stopped at a coffee shop on our way here." I glance toward the kitchen. Both Josh and Evan are busy making sandwiches. Josh is always up for eating. "I made a stew for us. And I brought you homemade cookies. Stevie made them for you. I hope you have an appetite."

"I will, especially for Stevie's cookies."

"She still has that dinosaur you gave her. She's given up most of her stuffed animals except for that one."

"The girl has taste. Just like her mother."

"More like her father, but I'll take the compliment." I take my seat beside his bed and make myself comfortable. "Stevie's doing quite well with her music. She has plans of becoming a concert cellist."

"She'll go far. And Jack? What's he up to?"

"He's got the music bug, too. He's formed a band with some of his friends. They're quite talented. I think they have a chance at making it."

"He's got the looks for making it as a rock star. Talent doesn't seem to be that important these days."

Jack looks like Quinn. There's no mistaking who his father is. I choose to ignore the barb sent Quinn's way. It's not his fault that he's drop-dead gorgeous and passed that gene on to his kids.

"David's planning on being a soccer superstar. He's twelve, so I'm sure his plans will change a few times before he knows what he wants."

Foxx nodded. "I wanted to be an Olympic swimmer. I just couldn't shave off one damned second."

"Swimming's loss, publishing's gain. You are an excellent editor."

"I managed to help a few books get on the bestsellers list and win a few prizes." He smiles with pride.

"That you did."

We fall into an easy silence once again. I think of Foxx and our sometimes-turbulent relationship. Foxx was my book editor and a friend I communicated with by email or phone more than in person. He was Rene's friend, too. He tried his best to keep her happy even when it meant using me. There were hurt feelings, but they became distant memories when Foxx stepped in when David entered the picture. He was a true friend to Rene by keeping watch over both mother and son. And when Rene had her terrible accident, Foxx was there to look after David until Quinn took his rightful place as David's father.

We spent one weekend together at this cottage. Foxx had invited the twins and me when Quinn's scandal with Rene had become too much. Foxx had offered me sanctuary from the paparazzi, and the twins had a few days of adventure. Foxx was incredible with them, quickly falling into the doting uncle role. When they cried for their father, demanding their dragon bedtime story, Foxx gave them a story about a dinosaur, peanut butter, and jam. When they found magic stones on the beach, Foxx was there to share in their wonder. And when I watched Foxx stand on the dock, naked and dripping wet from his morning swim in the lake, I marvelled at his body and wondered at the possibility of loving a man like him.

"You are the love of my life, Davina."

"Foxx—"

"I knew I didn't have a chance with you."

"I'm sorry."

"Don't be. I knew I'd have fucked it up with you if you'd been mine. I'm not the family-and-kids kind of guy. We both know that."

"I think you're wrong. You would have made a great father."

"Too late now for regrets."

Foxx smiles, and yet I can see the sadness in his eyes. He points to a table with a tray, a liquor bottle, and two glasses. "It's time for a drink."

I get up from my chair to pour our drinks. It's our brand of whiskey. Foxx introduced it to me years ago, and our shared secret has remained. Jack Daniels. No ice. I pour the amber liquor into the glasses, filling them half full.

I turn to face Foxx and see a slight sparkle in his eyes. I have noticed that sparkle before—when we have enjoyed something that didn't include Quinn. That look of victory or one-upmanship a man has over another, especially when a woman is involved. I will give him that victory. Who am I to deny him?

I return to his bedside and hand him his glass. "To what should we toast?"

"To friendship."

"To friendship." I take a sip from my glass.

Foxx takes a long drink and then offers his empty glass to me. "That should last me for the journey."

Tears come to my eyes, and I force them to stay put. I will not ruin this moment by crying. I place the glass on his bedside table, noticing an envelope with my name. "What's this?" I pick it up and show it to him.

"It's a copy of my will. It's straightforward. I'm leaving everything in trust to David, except for this place. It's for you and the kids."

"Foxx—"

"My funeral arrangements have been looked after. Josh knows who to call. I would like my ashes spread here if you don't mind. I have great memories of this place."

"Whatever you want. I'll make sure it gets done."

"I knew you would."

I'm falling behind. Foxx is going way too fast, rushing to leave me and this world.

"I'm not ready to let you go." I hear the words before I recognize the voice as being mine.

He smiles. "Now, you tell me."

He reaches for me, and I lean in to make it easier for him. He dabs at the tears I now have no control over. "I'm ready, love. Cancer's a bitch, and I wish it on no one. When the fight is over, it's over. I've got nothing left. It's time to go to sleep."

I nod my head. "When?"

"I'd like to see the sunset one last time."

Foxx

three

She's here. I breathe a ragged sigh of relief when I hear her voice from my cottage's entrance. This morning I let the doubt enter my mind, thinking that her controlling son of a bitch husband would prevent her from coming to me. She is strong, my Davina. She won't let any man tell her what to do. I hear that she has a bodyguard with her. It boosts my ego and puts a smile on my face to know that her husband still sees me as a threat.

I wait for her to make her way to me as I lie in this hospital bed in the middle of my living room. I run my hands over my head, smoothing down any errant strand. My face and body may look like shit, but my hair has retained its youthful ginger colour. She loved my red hair. I am thankful for small mercies.

Davina finally makes her way to me. Her smile lights up the room, and I try my best to give her a welcoming smile. It pains me to move a muscle, even smile—yet, she's worth the pain. She leans down to kiss my forehead. I inhale her scent and feel my body relax.

"I won't ask you how you are. Just promise to tell me if you need anything."

"I promise," I lie to her. Please, God, give me an hour with this woman, and I promise to go peacefully without complaint.

Davina takes my hand in hers. Her hands are soft and warm, and I take comfort in her touch. We make idle chat. It doesn't matter to me what we talk about as long as I hear her voice. I haven't eaten in days, yet I hunger for her company. Her presence sustains me.

"You're beautiful and smart, yet you have no concept of what you do to men." I offer it as a compliment because it's true. Her natural beauty and her purity of character draw men to her like moths to a flame.

She takes offence, and my heart breaks again because I am messing up my precious time with her while dying. I have forgotten about Guy Tremblant. The asshole tried to kill Davina's husband, and when that didn't work, tried to kill her. I close my eyes. I can't bear to see the pain in her eyes. I should die now, but I am a selfish man, and I want to live another moment in her company.

She returns to me, takes my hand, and suggests we start again with a clean slate. We won't mention the men in her life except her two youngest sons. I push the pain aside.

Don't fuck this up.

She is mine once more. We talk. That is, she does most of the talking, and I listen. Her voice comforts me.

"You are the love of my life." I have to tell her. "I knew I didn't have a chance with you." I would never have been the right man for her.

I've done it again. Shut the fuck up!

She doesn't laugh at me. Instead, she tells me I would have made a great father. She isn't lying. I can hear it in her voice and see it in her eyes. She sees deep into my soul, more than I would ever let myself venture.

I need a drink, a distraction from letting regret worm its way into my thoughts. It's too late now for everything I could have had. I remind myself that I still have this time I have with her.

Davina pours our drinks. I ensured I had a bottle of Jack Daniels to share with her. We shared our first drink many years ago. I tried to seduce her on a summer night here at this cottage with Jack Daniels and the call of the loons. I was a fool not to see her love for that man, whether he deserved it or not. Well, at least we have this as something we can claim as our own.

We toast to friendship because her friendship has been the precious thing I have held on to throughout these years. Lovers have come and gone. Fair-weather friends kept their distance once my cancer became too much for them. The one constant in my life is Davina Stuart.

I drink my liquor as though it's water, and I am a thirsty man who has come across an oasis in the desert. My throat burns as I force myself to swallow.

"This should last me for the journey." I hand her my empty glass.

Her eyes well up with tears, yet she refuses to let them fall. She is strong, my love. Her strength gives me comfort and the courage to tell her of my plans. I'm leaving everything to her and her children, including this cottage. I want my ashes spread here at the lake if she is agreeable.

"I'm not ready to let you go." Her voice is soft and low. Her eyes open wide as she realizes she has voiced her thoughts.

I smile. "Now you tell me." I reach for Davina, and she leans into me. My bony fingers brush away her tears. "I'm ready, love. Cancer's a bitch, and I wish it on no one. When the fight is over, it's over. I've got nothing left. It's time to go to sleep."

"When?"

I take in a breath and let it out. "I'd like to see the sunset one last time."

She nods her head and murmurs softly, "Okay." Her lips caress my forehead. "I'm here for you. Tell me what you want me to do."

Evan clears his throat, announcing his presence, and Davi doesn't move. She's not embarrassed by our intimate moment. My heart swells with love for her. It is I who releases her, although reluctantly.

I motion to Evan with my free hand. He makes his way to my bedside.

"Is it time?" I ask him, knowing full well that it is.

"It's up to you," he answers. "I've put another log on the fire. The stew is ready. We're wondering if Ms. Stuart would like to have something to eat."

She looks at me, accepting that I won't be joining them. "I'm fine for now," she says without taking her eyes off me. "You and Josh should go ahead and eat."

Evan nods his head. Before he leaves, he checks my vitals. I don't know why, but it's part of the protocol he has to follow. I'm sure my blood pressure and heartbeat tell him the same thing. Death is coming. Evan leaves us, and I feel my body relax once again.

"What can I do for you?"

"Would you mind holding me?" I'm not ashamed to ask her for this. Dying in her arms is all I have ever wanted since I learned of this damned disease.

"Of course."

Davi joins me on the other side of the bed, where there is room for her. She pulls the covers back enough so she can slide in beside me. Her arm cradles my neck, and she holds me close. Davina pulls the covers up to keep us warm.

I breathe in her scent once again. I let my breath out slowly. I inhale again, holding onto her scent for as long as possible, hoping it flows through my body.

"Do you believe in an afterlife or heaven?" I need to know what she believes. Maybe she thinks there's a place for me somewhere.

"I believe we live on in the memories of our loved ones. Is there a special place our souls go? It would be nice to know that there is a place. I think heaven is different for everyone. For me, I imagine it to be a place where I was the happiest I've ever been. I'll be with my memories of that place and maybe the people who shared the memory with me. My heaven would be reliving that experience every day without knowing that it's only a memory."

"What if there is no heaven, only nothing?"

"Then a peaceful sleep is good, too."

"No hell?"

I feel her shake her head. "No."

"Where do you think I'll go?"

She chuckles. "You'll be here, my friend, swimming naked in the lake, listening to the loons and drinking Jack."

"I'll be alone?"

"Only if you want to be. It's your memory."

"Then my memory will be of the weekend I shared with you and the twins. That was the best weekend I've ever had. It still brings me joy to think of it."

"Then that's where you'll be."

I gaze out at the lake. The dull haze of the day has given way to a clear sky, and I see the sun's red glow slowly setting behind the hills.

"Thank you," I murmur. "I love you."

"You'll be in my heart always," she says softly.

My eyes close, and I hear her say, "Sweet dreams."

Quinn

four

I arrive at the cottage in time to witness a gurney with a body bag wheeled to the waiting hearse. My wife stands on the walkway, watching the procession. She is not alone. Josh and another man each have an arm hugging her waist. I will forgive them for this transgression because she needs to be comforted. From this distance, I can see her grief, and it causes my heart to ache.

I turn off the engine, exit my car, and head toward the hearse. The back doors close, and the attendants step away. They glance my way. There is a flicker of recognition in their eyes. Their hesitation allows me time to put my hand on the side of the vehicle.

"Rest in peace, Foxx," I say softly. The man may have been a thorn in my side, but he loved my wife. I cannot fault him for that.

My attention turns back to Davi. She walks toward me. Tears well in her eyes. Tears I know she has kept at bay until I came onto the scene. I have come to comfort her and will do whatever is needed to bring a smile back to her beautiful face. I am her strength, her rock.

"Quinn," she says as her arms hug my waist, and she buries her face into the lapel of my jacket. She doesn't ask me why I'm here. I'm sure she knows deep down in her heart that I couldn't stay away once Josh called me. She is my only comfort, and I know that I am hers.

My lips brush the top of her head. "I'm here for you, love." My arms pull her in tight against me. "Let it all out if you have to." She lets out a single sob, and then her body relaxes.

She shakes her head. "I'm okay." My jacket muffles her words.

We don't move, not even to watch the hearse make its way down the laneway toward the road. I see Josh and the other man head into the cottage. We are alone, surrounded by silence. The trees and snow provide a perfect space for solitude. We stand here for several minutes.

"Let's go in," Davi says as she steps back from me. "There's coffee on. Are you hungry? We have chocolate croissants and doughnuts."

I smile. My wife brought her comfort food.

"Coffee and one of your croissants sound perfect."

Davi links her arm through mine as we make our way to the cottage.

"Foxx left this place to the kids and me. I want us to come here in the summer. I hope you can be comfortable here, Quinn. You'll love it if you give yourself a chance."

My wife is thinking about my hang-ups at a time like this. I can't be that much of an asshole, can I? She knows me all too well, and I feel humbled.

"I'll love it because you do. I promise."

I open the door for her, and we step inside. The cottage is warm and inviting. I didn't know what to expect of Foxx's tastes other than his taste in my wife. We take off our boots and coats, then Davi takes my hand and pulls me toward the kitchen.

"Quinn, I'd like you to meet Evan. Evan was Foxx's nurse. Evan, this is Quinn, my husband."

I offer my hand to Evan. His grip is firm. Impressive. "Nice to meet you."

"Same here," he replies. "We've got coffee and breakfast if you'd like some. The funeral home attendants arrived earlier than expected."

Josh busies himself at the kitchen table, laying out plates and coffee mugs. Davi slips away from me and fetches the coffee pot and a plate of pastries.

"Let's eat," she announces.

I take my seat beside her. This atmosphere feels strange to me—it's not heavy with grief. There is no sign of sadness on anyone's face, especially Davi's.

What have I walked into?

"Foxx had a good death," Josh offers as though he picked up on my confusion. "I'm not an expert on dying, but the way Evan and Mrs. Thomas were with him, I believe he died at peace."

Evan nods his agreement. His mouth is too full of chocolate croissant for him to speak.

I gaze at my wife and see her hold her coffee cup to her mouth longer than needed. She's lost in thought.

"Davi?" I put my hand on her shoulder.

She shakes her head and smiles. "He still loved me. After all these years." She turns her head and gazes at me with her deep blue eyes. "He was the second most stubborn man I have ever met."

"Who is the most stubborn?" I ask her. Our eyes hold each other's gaze.

"The love of my life," she answers softly. "The man whose arms I hope to hold me when it's my time to leave this earth."

We lean toward each other and share a soft kiss.

We've had this talk many times before when the shadow of death had threatened us. We know that one day one of us will have to leave, and when we do, we hope the other will hold us in their arms and offer the soothing words of love's farewell.

Foxx

five

It's a perfect August long weekend. The blue sky is free of clouds, and the temperature is just right, hot but not sweltering. A gentle breeze blows off the lake. I couldn't have imagined a better weekend.

Davina and her family have arrived at the cottage. The interior has had a makeover, a freshening-up with a few new pieces of furniture added to accommodate the family. The kitchen has more dishes and cutlery. A small table displays framed photographs from a lifetime ago, including one of Jack and Stevie with me on the beach.

I make my way onto the deck. The wood has a new coat of finish, and the furniture has new accent pillows. It looks good, as it used to a long time ago. I take it all in, taking a deep breath, inhaling the fresh air, the scent of the pine trees, and the smell of the lake. I listen carefully and hear the lap of the water as the waves roll gently onto the beach. A loon calls out its mournful cry.

I am home. I knew happiness here. I can feel it deep inside me—the peacefulness and the joy of being with nature. Should I have come here more often? Should I have tried harder? The answers to my questions do not matter. Not any more.

I hear Davina calling to her family to gather on the dock. The men wear khaki shorts and summer shirts. The women wear sundresses. Davina wears the floral sundress she wore when she first came here with me. She wears a sunhat to keep her hair from blowing in the breeze. She is as beautiful as the first day I met her.

They stand quietly, holding hands while Davina says a prayer for me and offers heartfelt words. Quinn hands her a beautiful wooden box made of maple when she finishes. She removes the lid and shakes some of my ashes into the lake. "Goodbye, dear Foxx. Sweet dreams."

Quinn takes the box and shakes more of me into the lake. "You were a good man, although a pain in the ass."

The others chuckle softly.

Jack takes the box from his father. He gazes at it for a moment, then shakes some more of my ashes into the lake. "Thank you for dinosaurs and peanut butter stories. Cancer sucks."

Stevie takes the box and says, "Thank you for our walks on the beach and stories about birds."

They remembered.

Lastly, David takes the box from Stevie and shakes the remainder of my ashes into the lake. "Thank you for being a friend to Rene and for looking after me. Thank you for being a part of our story."

Davina and Quinn put their arms around David, watching my ashes mix with the clear water of my beloved lake. Stevie and Jack join them.

It is getting late. The sunset is as beautiful as I remembered. I gaze once more at Davina. She turns to face the cottage, and I swear she sees me. My lovely Davina is looking at me with tears forming in her eyes. She smiles and blows me a kiss.

Farewell, Davina, farewell.

I am standing on the deck of the cottage. I breathe in the air, enjoying the outdoorsy scents I've always loved. I hear children laughing, and my gaze follows the sound. Davina is here with Stevie and Jack. They are gathering stones for building our castle. Today, our story will be about the knight, his fair lady, and dinosaurs who love peanut butter. We'll sit on the deck when we finish and watch the most beautiful sunset.

Recipes

Davina's Favourite Crock Pot Beef Stew with Dumplings

Ingredients:

- 2 lbs stewing beef, cut into cubes
- 1 tsp Worcestershire sauce
- 1 medium onion, sliced
- 1 or 2 bay leaves
- ½ tsp garlic powder
- 1 tbsp salt
- ¼ tsp pepper
- 6 carrots, pared and sliced or quartered
- 4 potatoes, pared and quartered
- 1 -2 stalks celery cut up
- ¾ cups peas
- 3 tbs all-purpose flour
- 4 cups beef broth

1. In crock pot, mix stewing beef with flour, salt, garlic powder and pepper.

2. Add all the vegetables except for the peas (add them later).

3. Add 4 cups of beef broth and Worcestershire sauce.

4. Add bay leaves.

5. Cook on high for 6 – 8 hours.

6. Make cornstarch paste or flour paste to thicken the stew to your liking.

7. Add peas.

8. Add salt and pepper to taste.

9. Add dumplings.

Easy to make Dumplings
   1 cup sifted all-purpose flour
   2 tsp baking powder
   ½ tsp salt
   ½ cup milk
   2 tbsp salad oil

Sift flour, baking powder, and salt together into mixing bowl. Combine milk and salad oil; add all at once to dry ingredients. Stir until moistened. Drop from tablespoon into bubbling stew. Cover and let simmer for 12 – 15 minutes.

Garlic Shrimp with Lemon & Parsley

Prep Time 10 minutes

Cook Time 5 minutes

Total Time 15 minutes

Servings 4

Author Albert Bevia @ Spain on a Fork

Ingredients:

    15 jumbo shrimp

    2 tbsp extra virgin Spanish olive oil

    4 cloves of garlic

    ¼ cup white wine

    4 slices of lemon

    fresh parsley

    sea salt

    black pepper

    smoked paprika

    crunchy baguette to serve

1. Thinly slice 4 cloves of garlic, thinly cut 4 slices of lemon and then cut them in half, finely mince a ¼ cup of fresh parsley and reserve a ¼ cup of white wine

2. Season about 15 jumbo shrimp that have been peeled and deveined with sea salt, freshly cracked black pepper and a kiss of smoked paprika

3. Heat a non-stick frying pan with a medium-high heat and add 2 tablespoons of extra virgin Spanish olive oil

4. Once the oil gets hot add the sliced garlic into the pan and mix with the oil, then add the shrimp to the pan seasoned side down, after about 1 minute flip the shrimp around and add the ¼ cup of white wine to the pan, the slices of lemon and half of the parsley, give the pan a quick shake and cook for another minute and a half, then transfer everything in the pan into a shallow bowl

5. Garnish the dish with the rest of the fresh parsley and serve with crunchy bread

6. Enjoy!

Baked Churro Chips Recipe

Ingredients:

For the chips:

4-5 pieces plain naan bread

½ cup salted butter, melted

cinnamon sugar

For the mocha fudge sauce:

1 cup granulated sugar

1 ⅓ cups special dark cocoa powder

1 Tablespoon instant espresso powder

1 cup heavy whipping cream

½ cup salted butter

splash of vanilla

For the caramel sauce:

¾ cup brown sugar

1 14-ounce can sweetened condensed milk

½ cup salted butter

½ cup half and half

splash of vanilla

1. To make the churro chips, preheat the oven to 375 ° Fahrenheit. Cut each piece of naan bread into 10 triangles. Brush each naan chip with melted butter and dip into cinnamon sugar. Place on a baking sheet lined with parchment paper. Bake for 16 minutes (flip the naan chips halfway through baking). Let cool.

2. To make the mocha fudge sauce, combine the sugar, cocoa powder, espresso powder, and heavy whipping cream in a saucepan over medium heat. Whisk until combined. Add butter and stir until melted. Cook the fudge sauce over low heat for 3-5 minutes. Remove from heat. Add vanilla. Let cool 5-10 minutes. If you won't be using the fudge sauce right away, store in a mason jar in the fridge.

3. To make the caramel sauce, combine the sugar and sweetened condensed milk in a saucepan over medium heat. Add butter and stir until melted. Cook the caramel sauce over low heat for 3-5 minutes, until it comes to a slow boil. Remove from heat. Add half and half and vanilla. Stir to combine. Let cool 5-10 minutes. If you won't be using the caramel sauce right away, store in a mason jar in the fridge.

4. Serve churro chips with fudge sauce, caramel sauce, and some fresh whipped cream. Enjoy!

Francesca Bean, author

Chicken Empanadas

Ingredients:

10 empanada disks
(I prefer the Goya brand in the freezer section), thawed

2 cups of cooked chicken, shredded or diced
(I baked mine in the oven with a little salt and pepper, and olive oil)

1 ½ cups of shredded monterey jack cheese

4 oz can of diced green chiles

½ cup of Red bell pepper

½ cup of greek yogurt (I used non-fat 0%)

1 tablespoon of cumin

1 teaspoon of salt

½ teaspoon of pepper

½ teaspoon of paprika

Optional: 1-2 tablespoons of sriracha for heat

1 Egg, beaten for wash

1. Pre-heat your oven to 400 ° F.

2. In a large bowl, combine chicken, cheese, green chiles, bell pepper, greek yogurt, cumin, S&P, paprika, and sriracha.

3. Take your thawed empanada discs and spoon about 2 tablespoons of the chicken mixture onto one side of the disk. Leave about ¼ inch clean around the edge.

4. Brush egg around the edges of half of the disc and fold the circle over top of the filling. If the filling is coming out the sides at all, gently stuff it into the empanada and make sure that the edges are completely sealed.

5. Crimp the edges with a fork and brush the top of each empanada with the egg wash. Bake for 12-15 minutes until the tops of the empanadas just start to turn golden.

6. Let cool slightly and ENJOY!

Food With Feeling, author

Pan Fried Spanish Cauliflower Tapas

These breaded fried cauliflower bites are a simple and tasty tapas dish you should make at your next get-together! Just a quick dunking in egg and breadcrumbs and a minute in a skillet and you are all done.   — JustALittleBitOfBacon

Prep Time: 5 mins

Cook Time: 25 mins

Total Time: 30 mins

Ingredients:

   1 medium head cauliflower

   vegetable oil

   3 large eggs

   1 ⅓ cups dried bread crumbs

   1 tsp paprika

   kosher salt

Notes

- Prepping the Cauliflower: The reason to dry the cauliflower so carefully is that the coating sticks much better to a dry surface.

- Sauce for the Tapas: Fried cauliflower is great served with Romesco Sauce or with a garlicky aioli.

1. Cut the cauliflower into bite-sized florets. Steam cauliflower for 5 minutes; then immediately plunge the cauliflower into cold water. Drain well and then blot with a cloth until they are dry as possible.

2. Fill a large skillet ½ inch deep with vegetable oil. With the burner on medium, heat the oil to 350·F. Turn the burner down to low to maintain the temperature.

3. While the oil is heating (it will take several minutes), take out two shallow bowls or pie plates. Break the eggs into one bowl and give them a quick mix. Pour the bread crumbs and paprika into the other and give it a stir.

4. To coat the cauliflower florets, dip them into the egg, allowing most of the egg to drip off - you don't want much egg on the cauliflower. Then roll them in the bread crumbs. Don't worry if the cauliflower is only partially covered. What you are looking for is a thin coating over much of the cauliflower.

5. In batches (3 or 4 depending on the amount of cauliflower), add the florets to the hot oil and fry them, turning them every so often, until they are golden brown and crisp, 2 minutes. With a slotted spoon, take the florets out of the oil and put them on plate lined with paper towels. Sprinkle with salt.

6. Serve while still warm from the oil or make them ahead and then reheat in a 400F oven until hot and crispy, about 5 minutes.

Flank Steak with Goat Cheese on Toast

PREP TIME: 10 mins

COOK TIME: 15 mins

SERVINGS: 6

Ingredients:

- 1 tablespoon smoked paprika
- 2 teaspoons red chili pepper flakes
- 2 tablespoons olive oil
- salt and freshly ground black pepper
- 1 ½ pounds flank steak (or skirt steak)
- 1 8 oz jar roasted red bell peppers, sliced
- 6 ounces goat cheese
- ½ cup fig jam (or your choice of jam/chutney)
- 1-2 loaves baguette

1. In a resealable bag, mix together the paprika, pepper flakes, olive oil, salt and pepper. Add the steak, seal bag and refrigerate up to overnight.

2. To cook the flank steak, heat a grill pan over high heat. Grill the flank steak, turning once, about 8-10 minutes total for medium-rare. Let steak rest before slicing.

3. While the steak is resting, slice the bread into thin slices. Toast the bread in the oven if you'd like.

4. Slice the steak very thinly (as thin as you can) ACROSS the grain. Top each toast with goat cheese, steak, a couple of red bell pepper slices and/or small spoonful of fig jam.

Jaden @ SteamyKitchen, author

book club questions

1. How did the book make you feel?

- Were you saddened by the story?

- Are you glad you read it?

2. What did you think about the story?

- Was the story believable?

- Which character did you relate to the most/least?

3. Which parts of the book stood out to you?

- What did you think about Quinn's reaction to Foxx wanting Davina at his death bed?

- Do you think Davina should have gone to be with Foxx?

Other books by

Deborah Armstrong

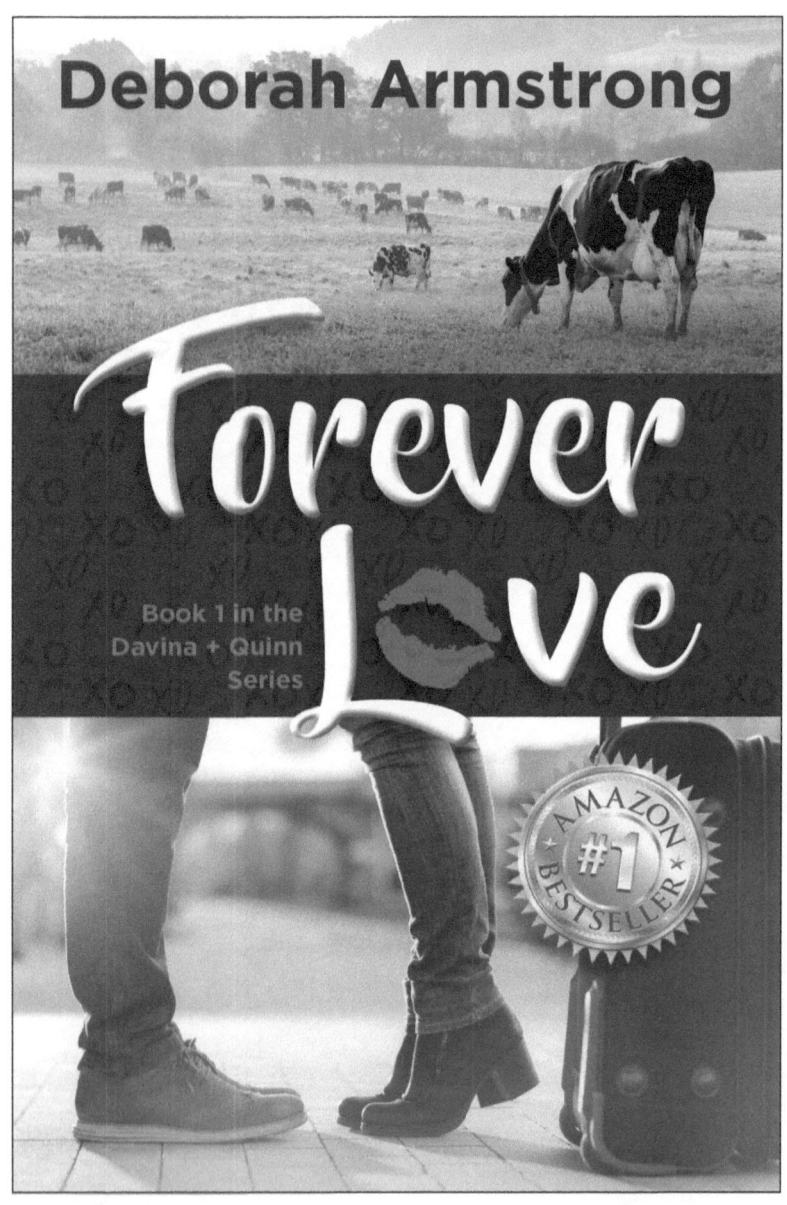

BOOK 1

Forever Love

What would you do if you found yourself sitting next to your Hollywood crush on your flight to Los Angeles? How would you spend those few hours? What if he asks you to go on a mile-high speed date with him?

Davina Stuart is a widow, dairy farmer, and bestseller author. She isn't looking for love, but she'll settle for a one-night stand with the handsome Quinn Thomas. What does Davina have to lose? Once her time with Quinn is over, she can return to her farm and get back to the life she loves.

However, Quinn isn't looking for a one-night stand. He's looking for his forever love, and he's sure Davina Stuart is the one for him. Quinn stops at nothing to romance the beautiful widow to win her heart. She may be older than him, but age doesn't matter when it comes to matters of the heart.

Join Davina and Quinn on their romantic journey with stopovers in Hollywood, New York City and Davina's dairy farm in Canada. Add an unplanned pregnancy, a stalker and a fortune teller who is never wrong, and you've got terrific romantic suspense for your reading enjoyment.

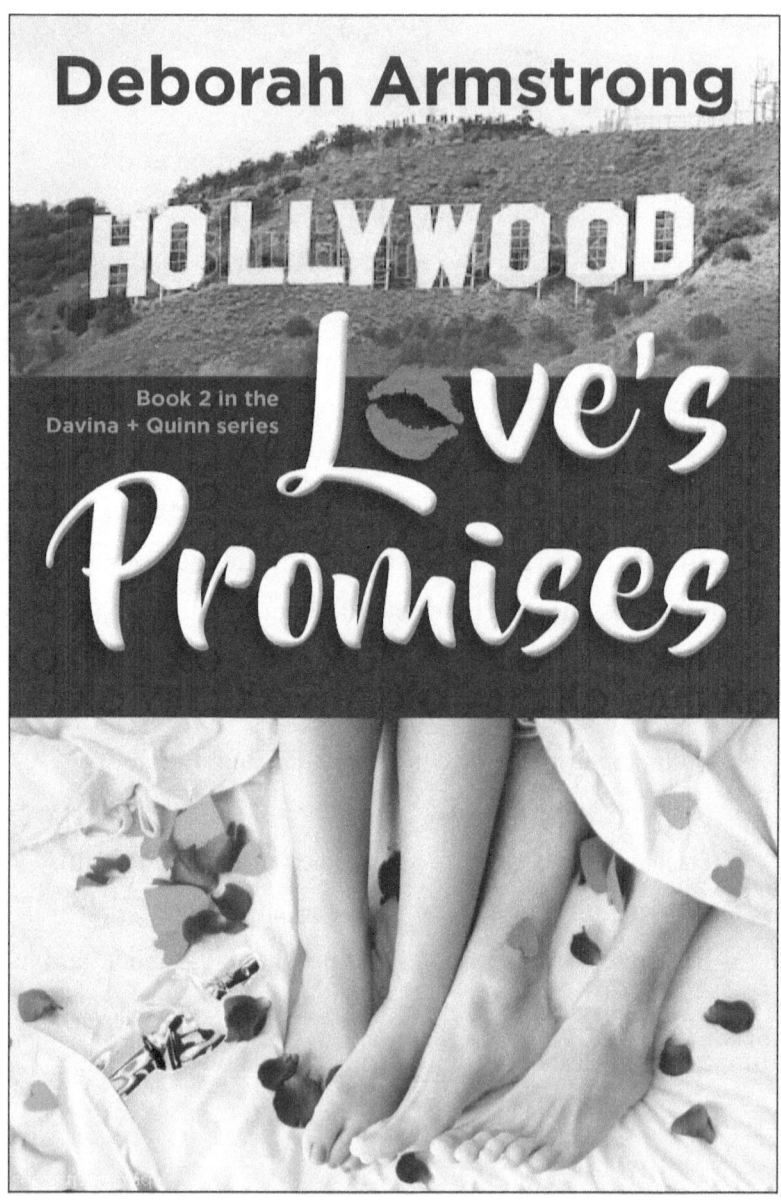

BOOK 2

Love's Promises

Davina promised Quinn her heart, and Quinn promised to keep Hollywood out of their bedroom.

The honeymoon isn't over, or is it? Davina and Quinn return from their hot and spicy honeymoon in Aruba and jump into Hollywood mode. It's time to promote Quinn's latest film, and Quinn's excited to have his bride by his side. Davina's thrilled, too, not knowing what to expect as the wife of Hollywood's famous movie star.

It's the premiere of *Lovestruck*. The lights dim, the movie starts, and Davina's world comes crashing down. Davina slinks in her seat as she watches Quinn break every promise he made to her with his body…with his eyes…with his kiss. How could he?

There's more. . .

Davina's pregnant, and the stalker is back. This time he's more determined to get what he wants. Nothing and no one will stop him. He's made sure of it. Will Davina and Quinn be strong enough to survive?

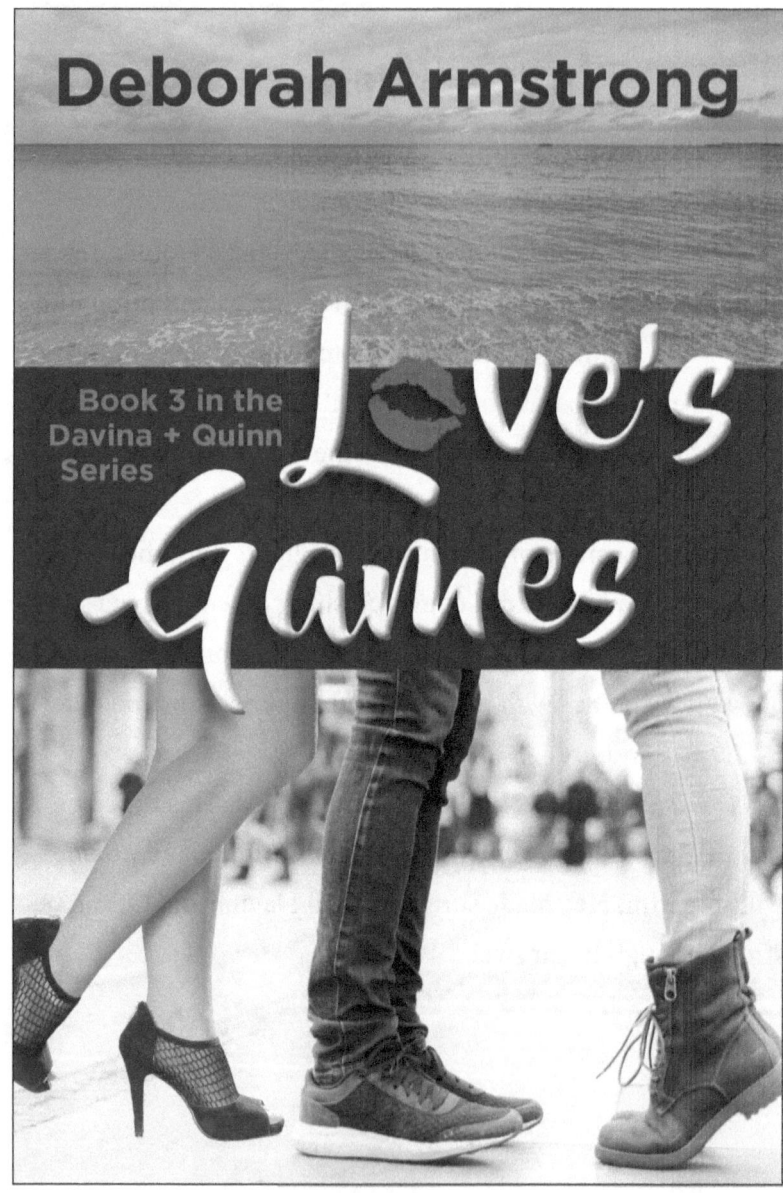

Deborah Armstrong

Book 3 in the
Davina + Quinn
Series

Love's
Games

BOOK 3

Love's Games

Quinn returns to acting after taking a leave of absence to spend time with his family. He loves living on the farm with his wife and kids. However, Hollywood is calling, and it's time for him to return to the silver screen.

Quinn's co-star is Rene Adams. In previous movies, they were known for their great on-screen chemistry. However, Quinn now wants nothing to do with Rene once the cameras stop. He has a wife and children waiting for him, and no one will come between them. Family means everything to Quinn.

Rene has a plan. She had Quinn in her bed before Davina came into his life. She can have him again.

Then. . .

A death in Quinn's family causes Quinn to play a game where the risks are high. He draws Rene and Davina into a game where losing isn't an option.

Davina doesn't play games. Quinn knows this but wants to test Davina's love for him. Will she give in to his demands? If not, is he willing to lose her and his family?

Rene loves to play games. Eager to win Quinn, she plays along with Quinn and adds a few moves of her own to better her odds. Will Rene's schemes get her what she wants?

What will come from Quinn's game playing?

BOOK 4

Love's Challenges

Jack Thomas is a rising rock star. He's got the looks and the talent. It doesn't hurt that his parents are Davina and Quinn Thomas.

He's on tour with his band, Dragon Slayers. The concert halls are sold out, their hit songs are at the top of the charts, and there's no where else to go but up.

Then …

Jack meets Molly at a coffee shop and there's an instant attraction. She has no idea who he is and he likes that. It's nice to not be known as the singer with famous parents. Jack invites Molly to his concert.

Molly arrives at the concert. She doesn't know what Jack's job is, nor does she know much about Dragon Slayers. She doesn't listen to much music.

The band comes on stage, and Molly quickly realizes who Jack is. He sings to her. She's pulled into the magic of his voice.

Until …

Jack takes off his shirt and Molly sees the monsters that cover his body. Tattoos. She can't bear the sight of them. Molly witnessed the murder of her father by a tattooed man, and the images have haunted her for years.

Now …

Jack wants to win Molly's heart. He makes it his mission to take away her fear of his tattoos. His tattoos have a story to tell her. One he's sure she wants to hear and see. If only he can get through to her.

Follow Jack and Molly in their adventure as they work on earning each other's trust, while Molly learns to deal with her fears.

Excerpt from

Deborah Armstrong

Davina + Quinn
a short story
Love's Embrace

Quinn

Stevie's light is on. I tap lightly on her door before entering. She's the night owl of the three, running on endless energy, much like me. Davi calls Stevie her little Bunny. She used to call me the Battery Bunny. I smile, remembering why.

"Daddy?" Stevie asks me when she looks up from her laptop screen. She's the only one who still calls me Daddy. I hope she never stops.

"Hey, Sweetie," I say as I make my way to her bedside. The dog and cat have beaten me to her.

"I miss Mom," Stevie says as she hugs the dog. The cat settles at Stevie's feet.

"I do, too." I sit on the edge of her bed and look at her laptop screen. She's watching *The Engagement*, a movie I made almost twenty years ago. "That takes me back. That was Mom's favourite movie when I met her. She said she fell in love with me when she saw it."

"She fell in lust with you, Daddy. You're allowed to say lust in front of me. I'm sixteen, you know." Stevie slides over in her bed and pats the mattress. "Watch it with me?"

There's no refusing my daughter, especially when I know she needs the company. I do, too. I'm not ready to go to bed alone. I place my drink on her nightstand and make myself comfortable on her bed, leaning my back against her padded headboard. Stevie adjusts the laptop screen so that we can both see the movie. She turns up the volume and presses play.

I remember when I first saw this movie with Davi. It was our first date. Davi insisted we dine in an outdoor restaurant that happened to be showing this movie. I complained. I didn't watch my films. Ever. But she insisted, and I couldn't say no to her. We dined on steak and drank single malt scotch. Seeing my unease, she leaned over and whispered in my ear that after seeing *The Engagement* for the first time, she went home and masturbated with her vibrator, giving herself one of the most intense orgasms she'd ever had. I choked on my drink, shocked by her confession. I'd never been with a woman who was so brutally honest and who could put me at ease so effortlessly. She knew what to say for me to let down my guard. If I hadn't known it before, I knew then that I would never let this woman out of my life.

"Daddy!"

Stevie's voice pulls me back to the present. "Uh huh?"

"What's it like kissing a woman who isn't Mom?"

Kill me now. Is Stevie asking me sex questions? Didn't Davi have *the talk* with her? She knows about the birds and the bees. We live on a farm. She's seen cows and cats give birth. What the hell am I supposed to say? I'm a shitty liar. All of my acting awards mean nothing when it comes to avoiding telling the truth to my family.

I know Stevie sees the fear in my eyes. She puts her hand on mine, a child comforting an adult. I am pathetic. "Daddy, it's not a tough question. I know you didn't know Mom when you made this movie. But what was it like kissing Rene and then kissing Mom?"

Oh, for fuck's sake. Stevie's asking me about Rene. The kids know about Rene. They know about David's conception, not about their father's fucked up plan that almost cost him his marriage. Why is she asking me about Rene now? I shift uneasily on the bed, looking away from the offending kissing scene on the screen. My gaze finds a poster of a unicorn. Why can't Stevie ask me about unicorns and if they are real? I could answer that question. Please, let's talk about unicorns. Stevie always asked me about unicorns—twelve years ago, when I wasn't so pathetic.

I look down at my daughter, relieved that her gaze has returned to the screen. I pray she'll let my silence be my answer.

"I'm waiting," she says with that perfect sing-song of impatience.

"I'm thinking."

"You're a terrible liar."

"Actors lie all the time. When we lie exceptionally well, we win an Oscar or two."

"Well, you're not winning one with this performance."

I'll be damned. My daughter has her mother's gift for putting me in my place. Her eldest daughter, Cat, has the skill, too. Come to think of it, my mother had the ability. I hate the women in my life. I'm a pathetic liar.

I take a deep breath as I find the right words to dig myself out of what appears to be a massive and dangerous hole. "Kissing any woman who is not your mother is like practicing for the real thing. It's not something I enjoy doing, but I have to. Think of it as though you're practicing the cello. You complain about having to practice your scales and studies, but you know the effort is worth it because there's a big recital waiting for you at the end, and you'll be spectacular."

"So you're saying that you kiss other women for practice so that you're perfect when you kiss Mom?"

I'd settle for that reason if it ended this conversation. "Yes."

"Liar."

She's got me, and I know there's no way out but to tell her the real deal. I reach for the laptop and shut the lid. Stevie shifts her body so she can look right up at me, her gaze showing her fully operational bullshit detectors, the same as her mother's. There's no way to escape.

"It's nice to kiss my co-stars. However, I can't say that I look forward to it. Every woman kisses differently; sometimes the kiss feels completely awkward and wrong."

"Like she's got nasty breath?"

"We all suck on a few mints before we shoot the kiss, at least we're supposed to. It's more like our mouths don't have the right fit together. Our teeth meet; we can't get in the right position; it's just bad."

"So, are you saying that's what it's like kissing all of your co-stars?"

"Not all the time. The point is that it's not something I look forward to doing. It may look like a lot of fun to make out with other women, but your Mom is the only woman for me." I can see by the expression on her face that she isn't satisfied with the answer. I'd left out one crucial part. "Rene was a great kisser when I dated her. When I met your mother, her kiss had lost its effect on me. When we had a kissing scene, I tried to get the job done in one take."

"Weren't the two of you known for your steamy onscreen chemistry?"

"It was acting. When a kiss is real, and it's with a person you truly like or love, it's the best thing ever. You can't imagine anything better than kissing that person. No one else comes close to giving you that perfect kiss. That's my opinion on kissing. Are there any more questions?"

Stevie pulls the dog closer to her for support. I know she's debating whether to ask me what is on her mind.

"Have you ever kissed a guy?"

"On the mouth?"

"Yes."

"No. I've never kissed a man on the mouth in real life or on screen."

"Would you? If a studio offered you a great role, but it meant you had to be gay, would you?"

I clear my throat before answering. Why? I have no idea, but it seems like the thing to do at the time. "Before accepting a part like that, I would ask your mother for her opinion, and then I would ask you, Jack and David for yours. I wouldn't commit to a role if it caused any of you embarrassment."

"So you think it's embarrassing to be gay?"

"God, no, Stevie. You know we actively support the gay community and gay rights. No one has the right to tell another person who they can love. I'm more concerned about the three of you. You're young. Your peers can be quite cruel, and I'd hate to think you got bullied because of a part I played in a movie."

"What if one of us was gay? Like me."

Her question hits me like a locomotive going a hundred miles an hour. I can feel the air in my lungs escape my body, and now I have to force myself to breathe while keeping my face in the best passive expression I can muster. I can hear a tiny voice in my head warning me. "*This is an important moment in your daughter's life. Don't fucking blow it. Damn you, man, don't blow it.*"

"Being gay doesn't change anything in our family, sweetheart. You know that our love for you, for all of you, is unconditional. We don't get to choose our sexuality. It chooses us."

Stevie falls into my arms and hugs me. "I love you, Daddy. Mom said you'd understand."

I kiss the top of her forehead. It's the only thing I can think of doing. My head is reeling. "So, Mom knows?"

"Yes. I didn't want her to tell you. I had to do it myself. You're not mad, are you?"

"No, I'm not mad. Why would I be mad?" The tiny voice in my head screams at me not to say it, but I ignore it because I'm pathetic, and a dad, and my daughter has just come out to me. "Are you sure? You're only sixteen. You've got time to decide."

Stevie pushes away from me. Her wide eyes flare brightly with a temper shared with her mother. "Did you have to think about whether you liked girls or boys, or did you just know?"

I shake my head, cursing myself for not listening to the voice in my head. "I'm sorry. It was a stupid dad question. I think I'm allowed at least one in my lifetime. What do you think?"

She smiles at me. "Mom said you'd say something stupid. I forgive you, Daddy."

I will have a long talk with my wife when she returns. I'll try to fit it in between several love-making sessions.

"So, do you have a girlfriend? Am I allowed to ask?"

"No, Daddy, I don't have a girlfriend, but there is someone I like. She's the accompanist in the music department."

"One of your teachers?"

"Daddy! No, she's one of the students. She's new. You haven't met her."

"Does she have a name?"

"Can you wait until there's something to tell you?"

"You mean something more than what you've just told me?"

"Yes, Daddy. I don't want to jinx it."

Stevie yawns.

"You need your sleep, young lady. How about we call it a night?"

Stevie nods her agreement and hands me her laptop. I struggle off the bed, suddenly feeling older than my forty-five years. I trade the computer for my scotch and place it on her nightstand.

"Sweet dreams, baby girl," I struggle not to choke on the words.

"Daddy?" she asks as I make my way to her door. "I'll always be your baby girl, won't I?"

I turn to face her, knowing she sees the tears in my eyes. "You will always be my baby girl, and there's nothing I wouldn't do for you. I'll love you forever. I promise."

"Love you back," she says before she turns off her nightstand light.

I leave her in the darkness with the dog and the cat to watch her while she sleeps. She'll be better company for them than I will. I know that sleep won't come quickly for me tonight.

If you're looking for a new series with sizzle, the *Game Changer series* is the one for you.

BOOK 1 : *Boss*

Dane Andrews, known as Boss to the men who served with him in the Canadian special elite force, has one rule. Never socialize with the women in his hometown. He can't afford to be attached to a woman, especially in his line of work, and most of all, he can't let anyone know about his work.

Until —

One night Jules Montgomery walked into his bar and needed a hero. Dane stepped in to be the man that the red-headed beauty required. For one night, he pretended to be her boyfriend. He kept her company, made her laugh, and made her forget the stalker who was after her. For one night, they pretended to be lovers.

Five years later, Dane is brain injured. He has a service dog to keep him safe, his best friend to watch over him, and a house-keeper who loves him like a son. Dane also discovers he's the father to a precocious five-year-old daughter.

Can Dane reunite with the woman who has haunted his dreams?

Can Dane break through Jules' defences and win her love?

Can Jules reconcile the man of her dreams is also the man of her nightmares?

about the author

Deborah Armstrong hit the big 50, and became restless and couldn't concentrate on much. Her favourite escape was to read. Instantly, her daughter's romance novels became the ultimate magnet. Hours were spent devouring them.

That was then ... this is now. Deborah turned her restlessness into writing hot and spicy contemporary romance with a touch of country.

Deborah lives with her husband and five hundred cows on their dairy farm in Ontario, Canada. When she's not writing or working on the farm, she enjoys reading, travelling, watching movies, and spending time with friends and family, especially her grandchildren. She also proofreads and edits for fellow authors. Her writing muse tends to run on the liquid side: strong coffee, chocolate milk, and single malt scotch in no particular order.

Thrice each week, the local gym beckons. Cardio means book thinking time for unravelling plots and conversations for her current work in progress.

When Deborah's characters talk, she listens. Not surprisingly, they decide when and how to tell their story, talking to her at the strangest times. When she's driving, working out, or trying to fall asleep, they whisper in her ear and say, "this is what needs to happen next."

stay connected

Deborah Armstrong is a storyteller, creating fantasies and weaving them for your reading delight from her farm in Ontario, Canada.

If you are in a Book Club, bring Deborah to yours via Skype, Zoom . . .or in person! Whether it's a hot and steamy summer day or one kissed with a wintry landscape, have your Club gather their favourite snacks and beverages and discover the Davina and Quinn series. Deborah invites her readers to follow her on social media and to contact her by email. To work with her, visit her website and subscribe to her newsletter.

Website: DeborahArmstrong.ca

 WriterDeborah

 deboraharmstrongauthor/

 DeborahArmstrongAuthor

 deborah_armstrong_author/

 author/show/6467157.Deborah_Armstrong